GRAND CANYON
A Trail Through Time

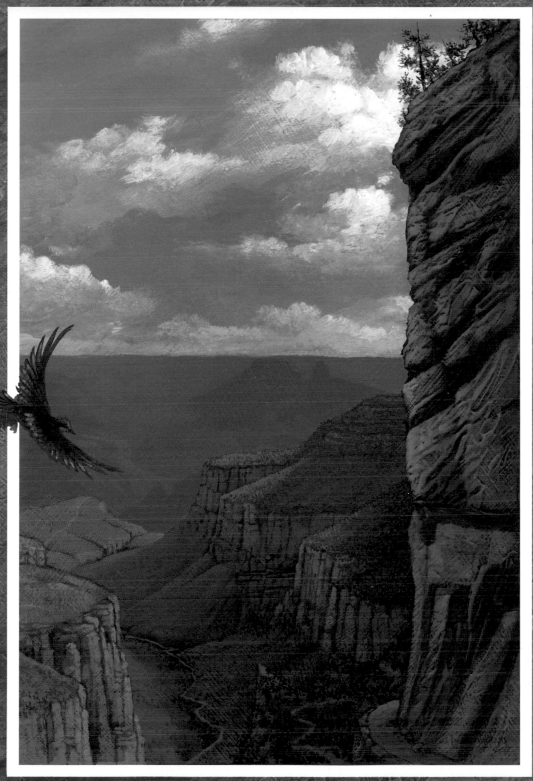

Linda Vieira
Illustrations by Christopher Canyon

Walker and Company New York

First published in the United States of America in 1997 by Walker Publishing Company, Inc.; first paperback edition published in 2000.

Published simultaneously in Canada by Fitzhenry and Whiteside, Markham, Ontario L3R 4T8

Library of Congress Cataloging-in-Publication Data
Vieira, Linda.
Grand Canyon: a trail through time/Linda Vieira; illustrations by Christopher Canyon
p. cm.
Includes index.
Summary: Describes the deep trench known as the Grand Canyon, found in the Grand Canyon National Park, and the activities of visitors to the park.
ISBN 0-8027-8625-1 (hc). —ISBN 0-8027-8627-8 (reinforced)
1. Grand Canyon (Ariz.)—Juvenile literature. 2. Trail riding—Arizona—Grand Canyon——Juvenile literature. [1. Grand Canyon (Ariz.)
2. Grand Canyon National Park (Ariz.) 3. National parks and reserves.] I. Canyon, Christopher, ill. II. Title.
F788.V54 1997
917.91'320453—dc21   97-156   CIP   AC
ISBN 0-8027-7569-1 (paperback)

Book design by Janice Noto-Helmers

Printed in Hong Kong

2 4 6 8 10 9 7 5 3 1

To my wonderful Nick, who gives me the
time and space to follow my dreams.
This one is just for you. —L. V.

Dedicated to Robert J. Pagels —C. C.

A predawn storm rumbles over Grand Canyon National Park. Cracks of lightning shatter the dark sky, flashing above an enormous plateau of peaks, valleys, and trenches where ancient mountains once stood. The deepest trench is called the Grand Canyon, one of the Seven Natural Wonders of the World.

5

Dawn comes, bringing daylight to spires and buttes standing like sentries on the plateau, worn down by weathering and erosion. Coyotes teach their pups to hunt for food in thick forests along the edges of the Canyon.

housands of visitors from all over the world have come to view the splendor of the Grand Canyon. In campgrounds and lodges near the north and south rims, they prepare for the day's activities.

8

The morning sun climbs above distant mountains, revealing cliffs hanging over the Colorado River at the bottom of the Grand Canyon. The river took almost six million years to carve the Canyon, creating a channel about one mile deep and more than 275 miles long. Wind and water wore down its steep sides, widening the chasm between the cliffs. A raven glides across the opening, making lazy circles over the river far below.

The sun chases away shadows on the craggy rocks
thousands of feet below the rims. Pack mules begin
a five-hour trip down to the deepest part of the
Canyon. They follow each other along a twisted,
ten-mile trail to the riverbed. Clouds of dust follow
them as voices from the top fade away.

12

anyon visitors along the trail peer with curiosity at symbols of people and animals that were painted on a boulder by Havasupai Indians long ago. Havasupai still live in the Canyon today, tending their flocks and farms in the summertime, hunting small game and gathering nuts and berries in the winter months.

15

As the sun moves higher in the sky, smaller side canyons with rocks layered like multicolored ribbons come into view. Bighorn sheep walk easily along the steep walls of the canyons, looking for food in hidden pockets of soil. Wildflowers stand around them in patches of purple and pink.

16

The mules continue down the trail to the inner gorge. They carry their riders past layers of rock that display millions of years of the Earth's geologic history. A canyon wren looks for bits of brush to line its nest, hidden in a rocky crevice just off the trail. It searches for twigs and grasses up and down the Canyon walls, flying past fossils of fish teeth and seashells.

19

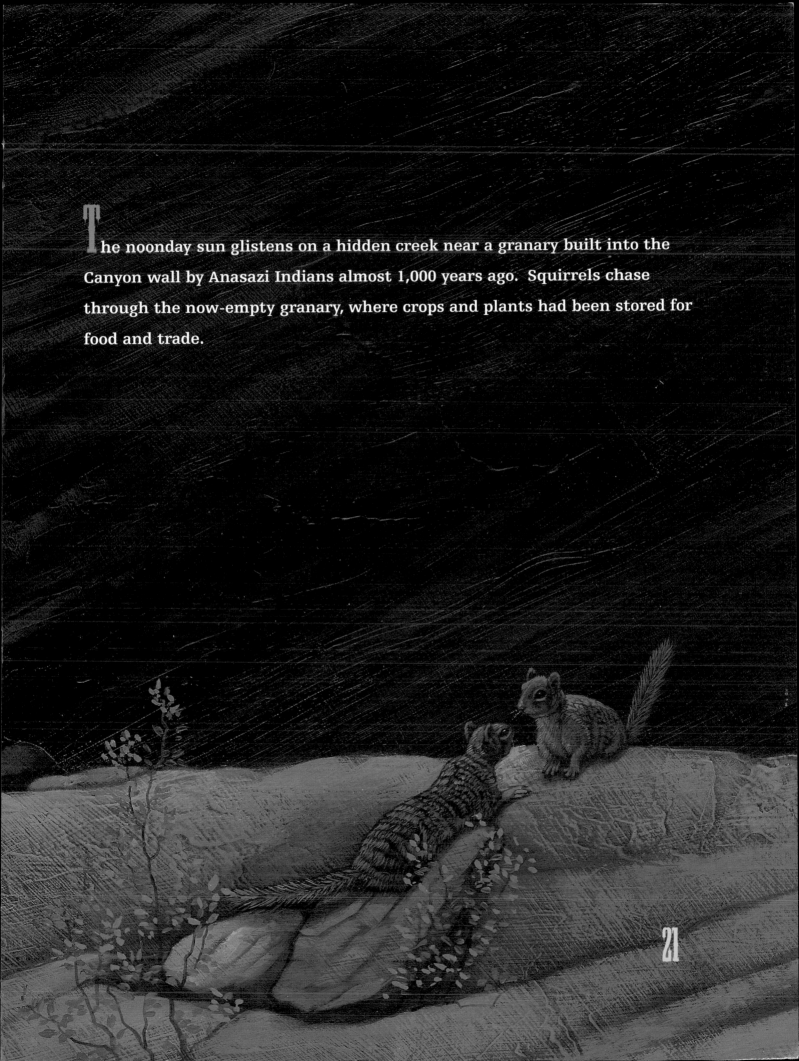

The noonday sun glistens on a hidden creek near a granary built into the Canyon wall by Anasazi Indians almost 1,000 years ago. Squirrels chase through the now-empty granary, where crops and plants had been stored for food and trade.

A lizard scurries off the trail. It climbs over fossils of prehistoric trilobites, embedded in layers of shale millions of years ago when the land was covered by a primeval sea. After the mules pass, the lizard creeps out from its hiding place to soak up the warmth of the sun.

The afternoon sun hangs low in the sky. A white-breasted nuthatch flies above beavertail cacti along the rocky banks of the Colorado River. Its song drifts over ancient pink, white, and gray rocks at the river's edge, the roots of mountains that stood there almost two billion years ago. The water tumbles over cascading rapids, while trout search for quieter streams in which to spawn.

A ringtail cat drinks from a slower side stream, watching for predators up and down the red rocks and along the river nearby. Laughter echoes from a bunkhouse, as weary riders and hikers share stories of their descent into the Canyon.

26

The endless cycles of eroding rock and moving water carved the Grand Canyon millions of years ago. Blustering wind and pounding rain continue to widen it, grinding down rocks that used to be mountains and volcanoes. The rushing Colorado River deepens this natural wonder, dragging rocks and mud along its path through ancient plains and lava flows.

28

The mules rest for the night in a corral near the river, awaiting tomorrow's seven-hour trip back up to the top. Weather and erosion make tiny changes every day in the rocky walls along the trail. Millions of years into the future, the same forces of nature will continue to reshape the Grand Canyon, digging even deeper into the history of our planet.

About 2000 B.C.E.: Archaic Indians crafted split-twig animal figures, the earliest evidence of humans at the Grand Canyon.

About 500 C.E.: Anasazi and Cohonina Indians migrated to the Grand Canyon.

Around 1185: Anasazi Indians built Tusayan Pueblo on the south rim of the Grand Canyon. Over 2,000 Anasazi sites have been discovered in and around the Grand Canyon.

1540: the first Europeans arrived at the Grand Canyon. Spanish Conquistadors of the Coronado Expedition stumbled upon the Canyon by accident while on their quest for the fabled Lost Cities of Gold.

1869: John Wesley Powell, a one-armed Civil War veteran, led the first documented expedition through the Grand Canyon by boat. The Powell Expedition is one of the great epics of the exploration of the American West.

1883: John Hance became the first nonnative resident at the Grand Canyon. This marked the beginning of early tourism and prospecting at the Canyon.

Mary Elizabeth Jane Colter, architect for the Fred Harvey Corporation from 1902 to 1948, constructed the Watch Tower at Desert View and other historical buildings in and around the Grand Canyon.

1919: the Grand Canyon was declared a National Park.

1919–1960: Modern tourism and commercial ventures developed in and around Grand Canyon National Park, including mule trips, raft trips down the Colorado River, air tours, and the building of lodges, restaurants, and campgrounds.